This book TALKS & ANIMATES!

Touch
ANYTHING
you see!
Here's
what the
buttons do:

Touch here
for VIDEO
fun!

LEVEL 1
Activity

LEVEL 2
Activity

Hint

Stop

Ready to start the fun? Turn the page!

Table of Contents

Join your favorite characters
as you learn about
how things work.

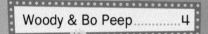

Disney · PIXAR

TOY STORY 4

Toys Save the Day

Woody, Bo, and their friends explore and use lots of things that were created by someone. This book will explain how some of those inventions work.

In Bonnie's room, the playground, the antique mall, and the carnival—inventions are everywhere!

WOODY

Woody is quite the cowboy. He's honorable, loyal and one of my oldest friends. When I first knew him, he led all the toys in Andy's room. He was Andy's favorite, and a favorite of mine, too. Sure, Woody's made some mistakes, but he always comes around and brings everyone together. And he never leaves a toy behind. Woody's always trying to do right by his kid. You gotta love him for it.

Bo Peep

Bo Peep is one of those friends that comes along only once in a blue moon. When she came into Molly's room, Molly was afraid of the dark, but Bo, well...Bo and her light made Molly feel safe. Bo always seems to do that. She solves problems and looks out for her friends no matter what.

Now, Bo is a lost toy and gets played with by kids from all over so she can help lots of kids every day.

5

INVENTIONS and INVENTORS

Inventions Are New Ideas or Things

When someone creates something brand new that has never been seen or used before, it's called an **invention**. An **inventor** is someone who creates new ideas or things. For example, German scientists made the first glue stick that twisted up like a tube of lipstick. They used an idea they got from a tube of lipstick to create a new way to use glue.

Some of the first toys invented were small clay marbles.

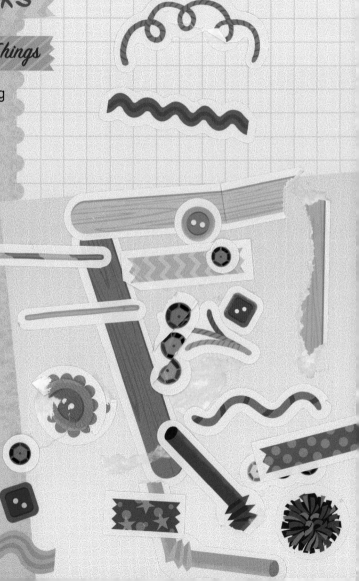

FORKY

Forky is Bonnie's newest toy. She made him from some arts and crafts trash in her kindergarten class, and then somehow, he came to life. For a while he kept throwing himself away because to him the trash felt like home. But after I explained, and explained, and explained how important he was to Bonnie, he finally got it. And now he loves Bonnie just as much as she loves him.

REX

Rex may look like a ferocious T-Rex, but he's really a gentle giant. He's always practicing being fearsome, and don't tell him I said this, but he's about as scary as a baby plush toy. Rex can be a bit jumpy, and he doubts himself a lot, but there's no better friend to a kid or a toy.

T. rex is short for *Tyrannosaurus rex* which means **TYRANT LIZARD KING!**

8

LEVER

Used to Lift or Move Things

Levers lift or move objects. When someone pushes down one end of a **lever**, the other part of the lever lifts or moves something. The push down is called a **force**. That force creates another force that helps lift or move the object on the other side of the **fulcrum**, or pivot point.

JESSIE

Jessie is one special cowgirl. In fact, I'd say she's the rootinest, tootinest cowgirl you'll ever meet. She's also the biggest cheerleader you could ever want. Whenever a toy or critter needs rescuing, Jessie jumps in boots first and gives it everything she's got. I'll tell you a secret, if you really want to see Jessie's heart flutter, set Buzz to Spanish mode and let him dance.

Jessie loves to yodel.

Yodeling is a type of singing started by goat herders in Switzerland hundreds of years ago. They yodeled to call their goats.

force

pivot point

CATAPULT
A LEVER USED TO LAUNCH THINGS

A **catapult** is a type of lever. Catapults launch, or throw, objects over a distance. If you place an object on one side and apply force to the other side, the pivot point, or fulcrum, sends the force in another direction and launches the object into the air. The more force you use, the farther the object goes.

11

COMBAT CARL JRS

I do love the Combat Carls! These fellas are lost toys who enjoy playtime more than just about any toy I know. All three—Combat Carl, Ice Attack Combat Carl, and Volcano Attack Combat Carl—can be pretty intense, but it's all to make sure the most kids have the most fun possible.

SWING

A Playground Swing is a Pendulum

A **pendulum** is an object that hangs from a fixed point and swings back and forth. The seat of a playground swing is held by chains that are attached to fixed points at the top of the swing set. When the swing is pushed or pulled back and let go, it moves freely back and forth.

SLIDE

A PLAYGROUND SLIDE IS AN INCLINED PLANE

An **inclined plane** is a flat surface that is tilted, with one end at a lower point and the other end at a higher point. Ramps are inclined planes. They make it possible to apply less force to push big objects up a slope, rather than lifting things straight up.

inclined plane

A playground slide is another example of an inclined plane. With a slide, the inclined plane is used to move something down instead of up. **Gravity** is the force that pulls someone down the slide. The steeper the slide, the faster someone will move, from a higher place to a lower place.

GIGGLE McDIMPLES

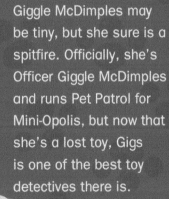

Giggle McDimples may be tiny, but she sure is a spitfire. Officially, she's Officer Giggle McDimples and runs Pet Patrol for Mini-Opolis, but now that she's a lost toy, Gigs is one of the best toy detectives there is.

BILLY, GOAT, + GRUFF

Ah, my girls, Billy, Goat, and Gruff.
They've been with me for as long as I
can remember. We were part of a
lamp together back in Molly's
room, and when our light was
shining, that little one always
got a good night's sleep. These
girls are my responsibility, but for
the last few years, they've been
looking out for me as much as
I've been looking out for
them. I do wish they were
better drivers, though.
They've crashed the
skunkmobile more
times than I can count.

Incandescent Light Bulbs
Uses a Filament

The lamps in the antique mall use **incandescent** light bulbs that turn **electricity** into light by sending an **electrical current** through a thin wire called a **filament**. The filament gets so hot that it glows and produces light inside the bulb. The filament needs to be protected from **oxygen** in the air, so it is inside the light bulb, where there is no oxygen.

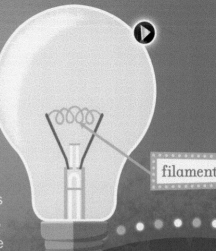

filament

Light-Emitting Diodes (LEDs)
Uses a Diode

LEDs are used in newer bulbs that require less electricity and can create a lot of light. An electrical current passes through the **diode** and creates light. LEDs last a long time, so they are perfect for lighting up a carnival.

Zip Line

Moves Someone From a Higher Point to a Lower Point

A zip line consists of a **pulley** on a **cable**. The zip line cable starts at a higher point and ends at a lower point. The person on the zip line moves from the top of the **slope** to the bottom, with the force of gravity. A zip line on a steeper slope will move at a faster speed.

cable

lower point

Duke Caboom is a
DAREDEVIL
toy modeled after North American
motorcycle stuntmen
from the 1970s.

higher point

slope

DUKE CABOOM

My friend Duke Caboom is a daredevil toy and Canada's greatest stuntman. We call him the Canuck with all the luck, though he's not always lucky at landing his jumps. He's really great at crashing though, which surprisingly comes in handy quite a lot.

BUZZ
LIGHTYEAR

Buzz Lightyear is my best friend and a pretty cool space ranger toy. He and I weren't always close, though. When he first came to Andy's room, I hate to say it, but I was jealous and a little worried that he'd replace me as Andy's favorite toy. Eventually, we worked things out, and I learned that when the going gets tough, there's no better toy to have on your side than Buzz. In fact, he's saved me more than a few times.

Pop Darts

wheel

FERRIS WHEEL

Uses a Wheel and Axle

spokes

axle

Ferris wheel seats are attached to the rims of the **wheel**. **Spokes** connect the wheel rims to the **axle**. Force is applied to the axle to make it turn. When the axle turns, the giant wheel turns. The seats are on the wheel, but the wheel would not work without the axle.

Bottle Smash

Star Adventurer

Duck Amuck

CAROUSEL

Carousel Horses Move at Different Speeds

Carousels move in a circle, around a pole in the middle. All of the horses move around the circle in the same amount of time, but the horses on the outside make a bigger circle than the horses in the center. So, the horses that are on the outside have to move at a faster speed to make it around the circle in the same amount of time as the horses in the center. Children riding on horses on the outside are moving at a faster speed and may get dizzier than children riding on horses in the center that are moving at a slower speed.

center pole

slower speed

faster speed

Ducky & Bunny

What can I say about Ducky and Bunny?
Well, those two are quite the inseparable
pair, and I mean that literally.

They're sewn together paw to wing.

Those fellas are a
hoot, and they're
always dreaming up the craziest
schemes. I guess that comes from
spending years stuck in a carnival
game. Now that they're free to
be played with by kids, they
couldn't be happier.

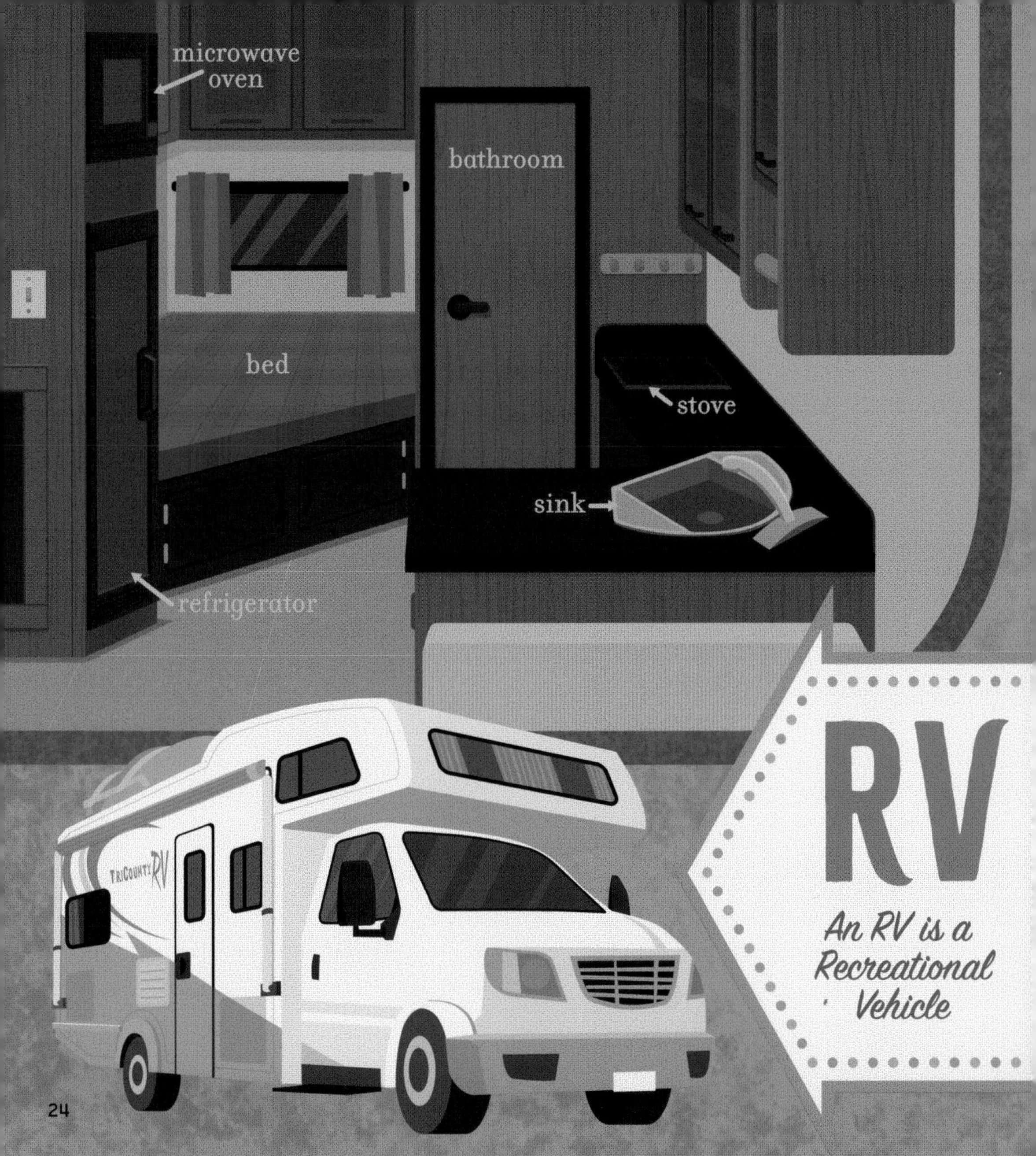

microwave
oven

bathroom

bed

stove

sink

refrigerator

TriCounti RV

RV

An RV is a
Recreational
Vehicle

Dolly

Dolly's the leader in Bonnie's room and wherever Bonnie goes, Dolly's there. Not being the leader was kind of hard for me to get used to, but I gotta say, Dolly does run a tight room, and all the toys respect her. She's great on the road, too. Bonnie had some rough moments on our RV trip, but Dolly made sure she got through them.

A recreational vehicle, or RV, is a large vehicle that people can live in, usually while they are on vacation. RVs have beds, bathrooms, and kitchen areas. They get power for microwave ovens, stoves, and refrigerators from plugging into an **electrical outlet** or using a **generator**. RVs pull water from different water holding tanks for sinks, showers, and toilets.

Trixie

Trixie is definitely the tech expert in Bonnie's room. She may be a dinosaur toy, but when it comes to computers, she's up-to-date on all those gizmos and gadgets. And Rex sure likes having another dinosaur to talk to. Those two can play video games for hours.

Global Positioning System
Made Up of Satellites

The Global Positioning System (GPS) is a way of figuring out exactly where something is. GPS has more than 30 **communications satellites** moving around, high above Earth. A GPS device is any device that is able to get information from the GPS satellites. When a GPS device can figure out how far it is from three or more of the GPS satellites, then it can show exactly where it is located.

Trixie is a *Triceratops*
which means
THREE-HORNED FACE.

GLOSSARY

Electrical current: An electrical current is electrical energy or power moving from one place to another.

Axle: A bar or rod that goes through the center of a wheel or group of wheels.

Electrical outlet: A socket that connects a supply of electricity to something that needs electricity.

Cable: A thick rope of metal or fiber.

Electricity: A type of energy or power that can build up in one place or flow from one place to another.

Catapult: A lever with a fulcrum, or pivot point, used to launch an object over a distance.

Filament: A very thin wire, thread, or fiber.

Communications satellites: Satellites placed in orbit around the earth to send and receive television, radio, and telephone signals.

Force: Something that causes an object to move, such as a push or a pull.

Fulcrum: A fulcrum is the point on which a lever turns or balances.

Diode: A diode allows an electrical current to flow in only one direction.

Generator: A machine that turns mechanical energy into electrical energy.

Gravity: The force that causes things to move toward the center of the earth.

Oxygen: An important part of the air that we breathe—we need oxygen to live.

Incandescent: If something is incandescent, it lights up when it is heated.

Pendulum: An object that hangs from a fixed point and swings back and forth.

Inclined plane: A flat surface that is tilted, with one end at a lower point and the other end at a higher point.

Pulley: A wheel with a cable wrapped around it that makes it easier to move heavy things.

Invention: Something someone creates that is brand new and has never been seen or used before.

Slope: An area or surface where one side is higher than the other side.

Inventor: Someone who invents new ideas or things.

Spokes: The bars or rods that connect the center of a wheel to its rim.

Lever: A lever lifts or moves objects. When one side of the lever is pushed down, the other part of the lever can lift or move something.

Wheel: A circular object that moves around an axle.

Disney · PIXAR

Join favorite characters from
Cars, The Incredibles & Finding Dory
in this LEVEL 3 K-1ST GRADE activity book.

LEVEL 1

PRESCHOOL

2-5 years

Teaches early fundamentals like numbers and ABCs, as well as shapes, colors & creativity.

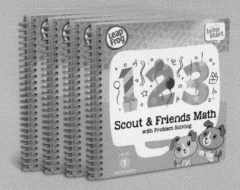

LEVEL 2

PRE-KINDERGARTEN

3-6 years

Introduces early key skills like phonics, writing, counting & critical thinking.

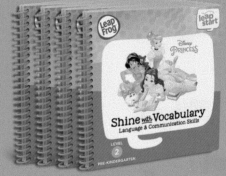

© Disney

LEVEL 3

K-1ST GRADE

4-7 years

Complements school skills like reading & math with life skills like logic & reasoning.

© Disney/Pixar